Odd Fish

Written by Fiona Undrill

Collins

We can go deep.

Odd fish are deep down.

This fish looks as if it has feet!

5

This fish is well hidden.

Look for its fin.

We go deeper.

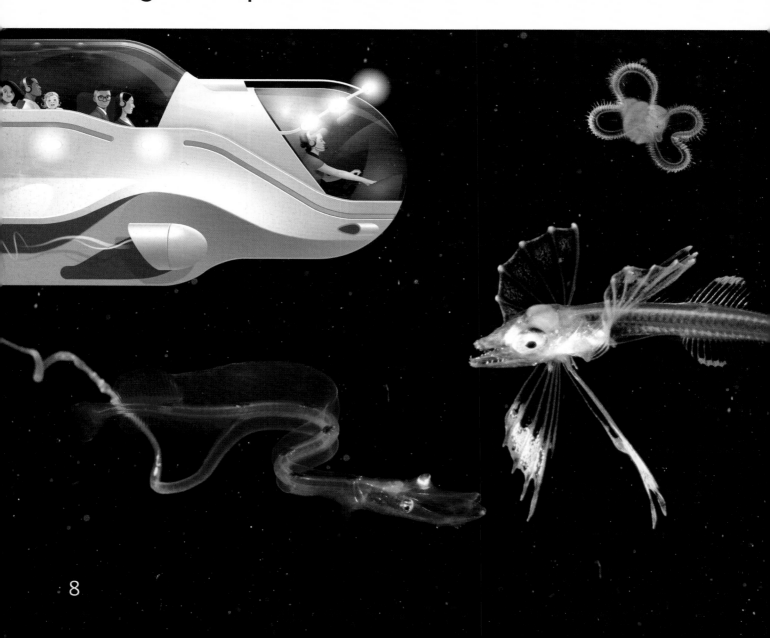

It is as dark as night.

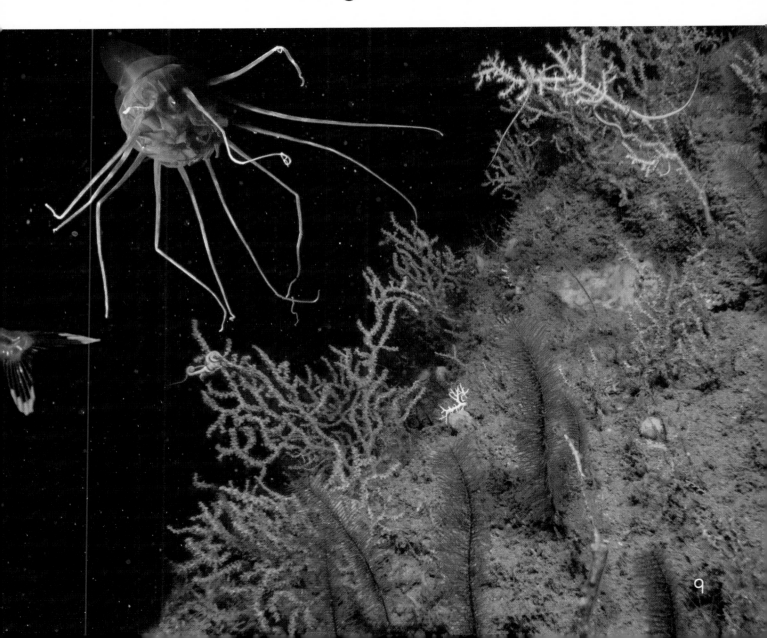

This fish has a light.

It winks in the dark.

This is a long fish.

It lurks at the bottom.

Look down deep!

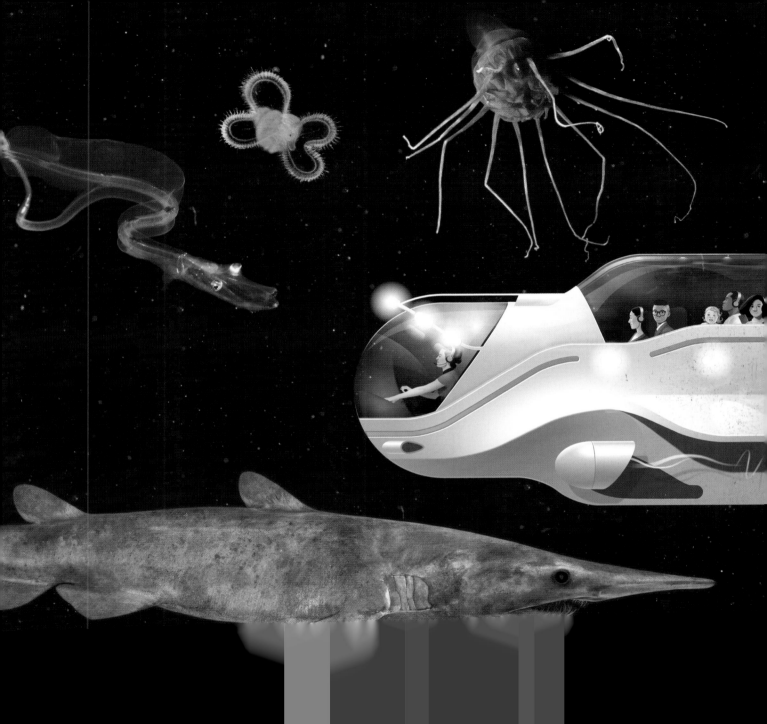

Review: After reading

Use your assessment from hearing the children read to choose any GPCs, words or tricky words that need additional practice.

Read 1: Decoding

- Remind the children that two letters can stand for one sound. Ask the children to sound out, then blend these words:

  d/ee/p   d/ow/n   l/oo/k/s   d/ee/p/er   l/ur/k/s

- Can the children find a word on page 10 in which three letters make one sound? (*l/igh/t*)

Read 2: Prosody

- Choose two double page spreads and model reading with expression to the children. Ask the children to have a go at reading the same pages with expression.
- Show the children how you read with authority and enthusiasm, as if you are a wildlife expert taking people on a deep sea tour.

Read 3: Comprehension

- Turn to pages 14 and 15. Ask the children to use the photos as prompts to describe the journey down to the bottom of the sea.
- For every question ask the children how they know the answer. Ask:
  - On pages 4 to 5, does this fish have feet? How do you know? (*It doesn't because the author only says it looks as if it has*)
  - On page 7, why do you think the author asks us to look for its fin? (*to prove it is well hidden*; *to show it is hard to find or see*)
  - On pages 10 to 11, why do you think this fish has a light? (*because it lives in the dark*)
  - What happens the deeper you go in the sea? (*It gets darker*)
- You can discuss the unusual names of the odd fish together. (cover and pp4–5: hairy frogfish; pp6–7: eyed flounder; p8, top: veliger snail larvae; p8 middle: swallower; p8 bottom: deep water dragonfish; p9: deep sea jellyfish; pp10–11: deep sea anglerfish; p12: goblin shark)